My First Worship

ISBN 978-1-64300-411-2 (Paperback)
ISBN 978-1-64300-412-9 (Digital)

Covenant Books, Inc.
11661 Hwy 707
Murrells Inlet, SC 29576
www.covenantbooks.com

My First Worship

Bruce D. Rose

Good morning to creation,
the sky, the clouds, the trees.
Good morning to the animals,
the birds, the squirrels, the bees.

Good morning to my mom and dad,
who taught me how to pray.
Good morning to my Father God
who's with me every day.

God gave to me a daddy,
to lead, protect, and provide;
and a mommy who will love me.
They walk together side by side.

He is the one who created me,
my God who made it all;
who loves me and who lives in me,
even though I'm very small.

God has given me friends to play with,
to laugh and to have fun;
to jump and climb trees,
to walk with, and to run.

God can use me to help them,
if they feel angry, sad, or afraid.
I can always be there to listen.
I can always be there to pray.

Mommy and me like to sing and dance
as she cleans and sweeps the floor.
I lift up my hands and sing real loud.
Me and mom love to praise the Lord.

Now it's time to rest, take a nap,
and go to sleep for a while;
and when I get up, I know I'll see
my daddy's great big smile.

I sit on his lap, and he'll open the Bible
and read all the stories God wrote;
how Adam and Eve lived in a garden
and Noah built a big boat.

My favorite story is when Jesus came
as a little child just like me.
He healed the sick; he walked on water
and made the blind to see.

He died on a cross and rose from the grave,
so I would be forgiven;
and someday soon, when God says it's time,
I will be with Him in heaven.

It's time to eat dinner, so we go to the table,
pray, and give thanks for the food.
We talk about the day and all God has done;
then we sing the song "God is so good."

Dad finishes the dishes, me and Mom sit on the couch and she holds me in her arms, sings and prays, "God, watch over my little one. Provide and protect, and guide with your loving hand each day."

Mom and Dad bring me to bed,
and I think of what I learned today;
that worship is not just singing in church,
but we can worship in so many ways.

Everyone's worship is different; we're not all the same,
but that's what makes God so great.
We all fit together like pieces of a puzzle.
We are fearfully and wonderfully made.

So I worship when I sleep. I worship when I play.
I worship when I give thanks to God.
I worship when I obey.

I worship when I sing and dance,
and lift my hands up in the air.
I worship when I'm in my room and only God is there.
I worship with my family. God gave them just for me.
God made me just for worship, and that's who I will be.

About the Author

Bruce has been serving as a worship leader for nearly three decades. He is currently serving as children's worship leader at Smithtown Gospel Tabernacle. He has been married to his wife, Colleen, for thirty-four years. They have two grown children Matthew and Amanda. Both are married. He dedicates this book to all his Grandchildren.

Also, a special thanks to Pastor Todd Marshall, <u>Worshipislife.org</u>

CPSIA information can be obtained
at www.ICGtesting.com
Printed in the USA
BVHW022105260220
573449BV00001B/11